This book is dedicated to all children.

Always have confidence in all that you do.

Small children like to
mimic their parents.
Give them something
good to mimic, read a
book.

Children learn what they live.

Morals are taught by parents from an early age.

They are not, learned from text books.

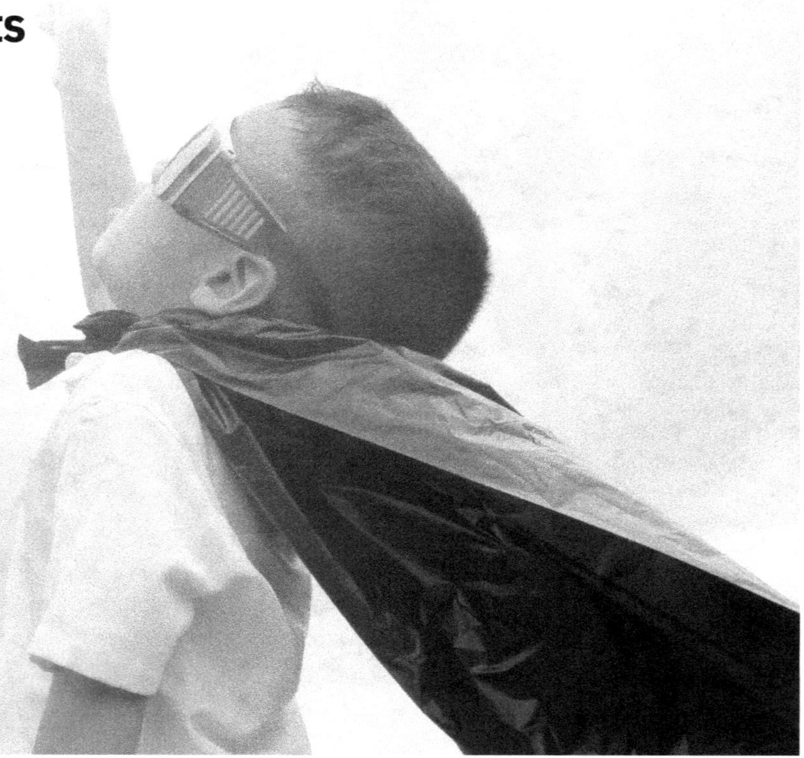

Buying a book for a child is a small price.
A smile on child's face is priceless.

Communication with children have better
odds in knowing what they want.

Using imagination can inspire us all.

Why not allow children to explore

their imagination?

A happy child is a child getting positive attention.

Taking time to spend with your child could
create the bond of a lifetime.

Being your child's advocate throughout
their school years could set them up for success.

An unfocused child can focus if showed how.

Reading bedtime stories can bring
enjoyment to both child and parent.

Children grow up so fast.

Cherish their early years

before the years pass by.

Criticizing a child once, could stick with them for years.

Too many unnecessary rules can
cause children to leave home early.

Giving a child a hug could

mean the world to them.

Praising a child will lead to self confidence.

Getting down to a child's eye level while
talking to them will help with listening skills.

Children that are given

tasks to accomplish

on their own will help

them with independence.

Helping a child have confidence can lead to great social interaction.

Ignoring a child's achievements
Can lead to a low self esteem.

A child is less
likely to lie if they
don't feel judged.

Letting a child know you are proud

Of them can send a feeling of accomplishment.

Inspirational thoughts all about Kids

Author: Cindy Roman